20 Minutes
Cookbook

Discover the Wonders of Quick Cooking in 20-Minutes or Less

By
BookSumo Press

Published by
http://www.booksumo.com

LEGAL NOTES

Table of Contents

Watercress Salad 30

Provolone Mortadella Sandwiches 31

Nutmeg Beef and Plantain Kabobs 32

Jerk Flounder Fillets with Mango Sauce 33

Nutty Pineapple Rice Pudding 34

Jerk Shrimp Soup 35

Kabobs Kingston 36

Tropical Seafood Skillet 37

New Age Lemonade 38

Shrimp and Fruit Lunch Wraps 39

Sweetened Condensed Milkshake 40

Southern Papaya Starter 41

Sanibel Island Parfaits 42

Peach and Papaya Sorbet 43

Bangkok Curry Stir Fry 44

Nutty Chicken and Carrot Stir Fry 45

Cookout Bananas 46

Yellow Jacket Crepes 47

Skillet Buttery Bananas 48

Colada Skillet Bananas 49

Fresh Spinach, Mango, and Coconut Smoothie 50

Greek Yogurt and Granola Bowl 51

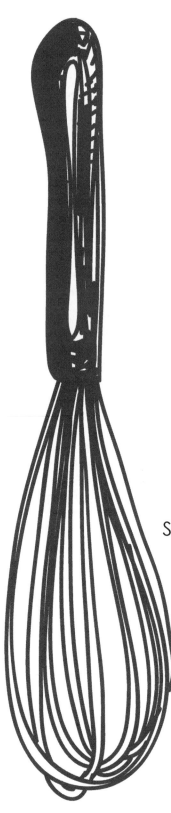

How
to Scramble Eggs

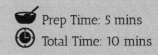 Prep Time: 5 mins

Total Time: 10 mins

Servings per Recipe: 1

Calories	420 kcal
Fat	33.1 g
Carbohydrates	9.7g
Protein	23.1 g
Cholesterol	575 mg
Sodium	755 mg

Ingredients

3 large eggs
1 pinch red pepper flakes
9 cherry tomatoes, halved
2 tbsps crumbled feta cheese

1 tbsp very thinly sliced fresh basil leaves
olive oil
1 pinch sea salt

Directions

1. Get a bowl and evenly mix the following: basil, eggs, feta, red pepper flakes, and tomatoes.
2. Fry in hot olive oil for a few secs without any stirring so the eggs set. Then begin to scramble them for 1 min.
3. Ideally you want your eggs to be only lightly set. Remove them from the heat. Season with salt.
4. Enjoy..

MEXICAN
Mornings (Scrambled Eggs with Corn Tortillas)

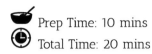 Prep Time: 10 mins

Total Time: 20 mins

Servings per Recipe: 6

Calories	283 kcal
Fat	12.2 g
Cholesterol	196 mg
Sodium	661 mg
Carbohydrates	30.8 g
Protein	12.1 g
Fiber	2 g

Ingredients

1 tbsp butter
1 (4 oz.) can chopped green chilis
1/2 tomato, chopped
6 large eggs
1/4 cup crushed tortilla chips, or to taste

1/4 cup shredded sharp Cheddar cheese
6 (8 inch) flour tortillas
6 tbsps taco sauce (enchilada sauce), to taste (optional)

Directions

1. Cook tomato and green chili in hot oil butter for about five minutes before adding eggs and cooking for another 3 minutes.
2. Now add some tortilla chips over the eggs and mix well before turning off the heat and adding cheese.
3. Now cover the pan and let the cheese melt down and the eggs get tender.
4. Get tortillas warm in a microwave for about 30 seconds and fold them around the egg mixture you just prepared.
5. Put some taco sauce over it before serving.
6. Enjoy.

How
to Make Porridge

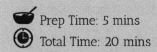 Prep Time: 5 mins

Total Time: 20 mins

Servings per Recipe: 4
Calories	507 kcal
Fat	20.5 g
Carbohydrates	64.2 g
Protein	19.2 g
Cholesterol	151 mg
Sodium	237 mg

Ingredients

3 C. water
1 C. powdered milk
1 1/2 C. rolled oats
1/2 tsp ground cinnamon
1/2 C. raisins
1/2 tsp vanilla extract
3 eggs

4 tsps butter
1 C. milk
3 tbsps honey

Directions

1. Get some water boiling then combine in your cinnamon, powdered milk, and oats. Once boiling again lower the heat and let the contents simmer for 12 mins.

2. Shut off the heat and add in your vanilla and raisins.

3. One by one add your eggs and make sure to stir them in completely.

4. Enter your porridge into a bowl and garnish each with some honey, 1 tsp of butter, and one fourth C. of milk.

5. Enjoy.:

TEXAS
Cajun Egg Sandwich Breakfast

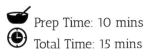 Prep Time: 10 mins

Total Time: 15 mins

Servings per Recipe: 1

Calories	471 kcal
Fat	31.5 g
Carbohydrates	29.6 g
Protein	18.1 g
Cholesterol	248 mg
Sodium	996 mg

Ingredients

1 tbsp butter
1 egg
1 slice Cheddar cheese
1 tsp mayonnaise, or to taste
1 tsp mustard, or to taste
1 tsp ketchup, or to taste
1 pinch Cajun seasoning, or to taste

1 dash hot pepper sauce (such as Tabasco(R))
2 slices white bread, toasted
1 lettuce leaf
1 slice tomato

Directions

1. Fry your egg for 3 mins in butter then flip it.
2. Top the egg with the cheese and cook everything until the cheese melts for about 3 more mins. Then add your Cajun seasoning.
3. Coat both your bread pieces with: ketchup, mustard, and mayo.
4. Layer a piece of tomato and some lettuce on a piece of bread then put the egg on top and add some hot sauce.
5. Add a bit more Cajun spice and add the other piece of bread to from a sandwich.
6. Enjoy.

Welsh
Toast Topping

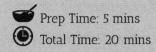 Prep Time: 5 mins
Total Time: 20 mins

Servings per Recipe: 6
Calories	333 kcal
Fat	24.6 g
Carbohydrates	12.6 g
Protein	15.3 g
Cholesterol	75 mg
Sodium	577 mg

Ingredients

4 tbsps butter
1/2 C. all-purpose flour
1/2 tsp salt
1/8 tsp dry mustard
1/8 tsp cayenne pepper

2 C. milk
1 tsp Worcestershire sauce
2 C. shredded sharp Cheddar cheese

Directions

1. In a big pot combine the following in melted butter: pepper, milk, flour, mustard, Worcestershire, and salt.
2. Stir and heat the contents for 10 mins with a low level of heat. Now add your cheese and let it melt nicely.
3. Enjoy this topping on some toasted rye bread.

BREAKFAST
Tacos From Mexico

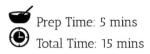
Prep Time: 5 mins
Total Time: 15 mins

Servings per Recipe: 4
Calories	537 kcal
Fat	34.1 g
Cholesterol	343 mg
Sodium	1298 mg
Carbohydrates	27.7 g
Protein	30.6 g
Fiber	3.9 g

Ingredients

6 oz. chorizo sausage, optional
8 (6 inch) corn tortillas
6 eggs
1/4 cup milk
1/2 tsp pepper
1/2 tsp salt

1 cup shredded Monterey Jack cheese
1 dash hot pepper sauce (e.g. Tabasco™), or to taste
1/2 cup salsa

Directions

1. Cook crumbled sausage in a pan at medium heat until golden brown in color.
2. Heat up two different pans at high heat and medium heat.
3. Whisk together eggs, pepper and salt in a bowl, and pour these eggs into the pan at medium heat.
4. Cook until you see that the eggs are firm and continue cooking after adding sausage.
5. Warm up some tortillas in the pan which is at high heat for about 45 seconds each side and add some cheese before filling with the egg and tortilla mixture you have prepared.
6. Also add some hot pepper sauce and salsa according to your taste before serving it.
7. Enjoy..

Autumn
October Oatmeal

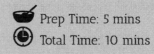 Prep Time: 5 mins

Total Time: 10 mins

Servings per Recipe: 1

Calories	594 kcal
Fat	31.9 g
Carbohydrates	67.6 g
Protein	18 g
Cholesterol	10 mg
Sodium	198 mg

Ingredients

1 (1 oz.) packet instant oatmeal, unsweetened
1/2 C. hot milk or water
1 tbsp almond butter
1 red apple, cored and roughly chopped

1/4 C. whole natural almonds
1/2 tsp cinnamon
2 tsps honey

Directions

1. Heat your milk in the microwave or a small saucepan.
2. Put your oatmeal in the same bowl that you will eat out of. Then cover it with the milk and almond butter.
3. Add in your almonds, honey, apples, and cinnamon.
4. Enjoy

EASY
South American Style Oats for Breakfast

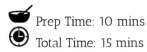 Prep Time: 10 mins
Total Time: 15 mins

Servings per Recipe: 2
Calories   220 kcal
Fat   5.1 g
Carbohydrates   35.2 g
Protein   8.7 g
Cholesterol   15 mg
Sodium   270 mg

Ingredients

1 1/2 C. milk
1/2 C. quick cooking oats
2 tbsps white sugar
1/4 tsp ground cinnamon

1 pinch ground nutmeg
1 pinch salt

Directions

1. For 4 min simply boil all the ingredients. Enjoy warm..

Rolled Oats and Almond Milk

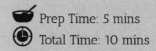 Prep Time: 5 mins

Total Time: 10 mins

Servings per Recipe: 4

Calories	266 kcal
Fat	4.9 g
Carbohydrates	53.1 g
Protein	6.5 g
Cholesterol	< 1 mg
Sodium	206 mg

Ingredients

2 C. rolled oats
3 1/2 C. sweetened vanilla almond milk
1/8 tsp salt

1/2 C. dried tart cherries

Directions

1. Microwave all the ingredients except the cherries for 4 mins.
2. Stir the contents at 2 mins.
3. Before serving the oatmeal add in your cherries.
4. Enjoy.

COCOA
Wet Oats

Prep Time: 10 mins
Total Time: 15 mins

Servings per Recipe: 2

Calories	516 kcal
Fat	9.1 g
Carbohydrates	108.1 g
Protein	6.9 g
Cholesterol	0 mg
Sodium	319 mg

Ingredients

2 C. boiling water
1 C. rolled oats
1/4 tsp salt
1/2 C. brown sugar

1 banana, mashed
1/4 C. semisweet chocolate chips

Directions

1. For 6 mins boil your oats in salted water. Turn off the heat and place a lid on the pot. Let the contents sit for about 4 more mins to get thick.
2. Add your chocolate, bananas, and sugar before serving and stir the contents.
3. Enjoy..

Buttery Eggs

 Prep Time: 10 mins
🕐 Total Time: 20 mins

Servings per Recipe: 3
Calories	311 kcal
Fat	20.9 g
Carbohydrates	12.4 g
Protein	18.6 g
Cholesterol	405 mg
Sodium	261 mg

Ingredients

6 eggs
2 tbsps butter
2 tbsps all-purpose flour
2 cups milk

1/8 tsp ground white pepper, if desired
salt and pepper to taste

Directions

1. Get a big saucepan and fill it with water. Add your eggs to the water and bring it to a rolling boil. Once boiling for about a minute then remove the pan from the heat and place a lid on it. Let it stand for about 13 mins.
2. After 13 mins take out the eggs, remove the shells, and dice them.
3. Now drain the saucepan of its water and melt some butter in it. Once the butter is melted add some flour and heat it until a ball-like shape begins to form. Then add in your milk and lightly stir until the sauce begins to boil.
4. While boiling add in: salt, white pepper, chopped eggs, and black pepper. Heat everything up then remove it all from the heat.
5. Enjoy with your favorite toasted bread.

TOMATO
Feta Eggs

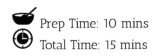

Prep Time: 10 mins
Total Time: 15 mins

Servings per Recipe: 4
Calories	116 kcal
Fat	8.9 g
Carbohydrates	2 g
Protein	7.2 g
Cholesterol	198 mg
Sodium	435 mg

Ingredients

1 tbsp butter
1/4 cup chopped onion
4 eggs, beaten
1/4 cup chopped tomatoes

2 tbsps crumbled feta cheese
salt and pepper to taste

Directions

1. Fry onions until see-through, in butter, in a frying pan. Then mix in your eggs. While the eggs are frying make sure to stir them so that they become scrambled.
2. Before the eggs are completely cooked add in your pepper and salt, then your feta, and finally your tomatoes.
3. Continue to let the eggs fry until the feta melts..

Egg
Salad

Prep Time: 10 mins
Total Time: 10 mins

Servings per Recipe: 8
Calories	83 kcal
Fat	5.3 g
Carbohydrates	1.3g
Protein	6.8 g
Cholesterol	212 mg
Sodium	141 mg

Ingredients

8 hard-cooked eggs, chopped
1/4 cup plain fat-free yogurt
1 tbsp parsley flakes
1/4 tsp onion powder

1/4 tsp paprika
1/4 tsp salt

Directions

1. To make this salad get a bowl: and combine all the ingredients until completely smooth and even.
2. Enjoy with toasted bread.

3-INGREDIENT
Fruit Banana Pancakes

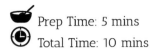 Prep Time: 5 mins
Total Time: 10 mins

Servings per Recipe: 2
Calories	93 kcal
Fat	2.7 g
Carbohydrates	14.9 g
Protein	3.8 g
Cholesterol	93 mg
Sodium	36 mg

Ingredients

1 banana, mashed
1 egg
1 tsp arrowroot powder

Directions

1. In a blender, add the banana, egg and arrowroot powder and pulse till well combined.
2. Heat a griddle on medium heat.
3. Place half of the mixture into the griddle and cook for about 2-3 minutes per side.
4. Repeat with the remaining mixture.

The No-Fry
Frittata

🥣 Prep Time: 3 mins
🕐 Total Time: 6 mins

Servings per Recipe: 1
Calories	434.7 kcal
Cholesterol	435.5mg
Sodium	868.6mg
Carbohydrates	13.2g
Protein	38.8g

Ingredients

2 eggs
1/4 C. fat-free evaporated milk
1/2 C. fresh spinach leaves, stems removed, cleaned, dried, ribbed into small pieces
1 roma tomato

1 slice turkey bacon
1/3 C. shredded part-skim mozzarella cheese
nonstick spray
salt and pepper

Directions

1. Get a bowl and coat it with nonstick spray. Then add in your spinach.
2. Now dice your tomatoes and add them in as well then add the bacon and the cheese over everything.
3. Whisk two eggs and the milk in a small bowl then add them to the spinach mix.
4. Now add some pepper and salt.
5. Place everything in the microwave for 3 mins on the highest power setting.
6. Enjoy.

SPICED
Kale Ceviche

Prep Time: 10 mins
Total Time: 10 mins

Servings per Recipe: 6
Calories	117.8
Fat	6.3g
Cholesterol	0.0mg
Sodium	121.6mg
Carbohydrates	15.7g
Protein	2.6g

Ingredients

1 bunch kale, leaves
1 large avocado, peeled
1 tbsp lemon juice
1/4 tsp salt
1/2 tsp crushed red pepper flakes

1/2 red bell pepper
1 small carrot, grated
1/2 purple onion, chopped
1 1/2 C. mandarin orange segments

Directions

1. Get a mixing bowl: Toss in it the kale with avocado, lemon juice, salt and red pepper flakes.
2. Mix them well with your hands until they avocado become mashed and smooth.
3. Add the rest of the ingredients. Toss them to coat.
4. Chill your ceviche in the fridge for 35 min then serve it.
5. Enjoy.

Ceviche Cups

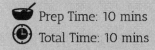

Prep Time: 10 mins
Total Time: 10 mins

Servings per Recipe: 4
Calories	278.8
Fat	15.1g
Cholesterol	37.4mg
Sodium	346.6mg
Carbohydrates	15.1g
Protein	23.6g

Ingredients

2 (6 oz.) cans albacore tuna in water, drained
1/2 C. sweet onion, diced
1 large tomatoes, seeded and diced
1 small cucumber, peeled and diced
1/4 C. cilantro,
1 - 2 serrano chili, diced

2 - 3 limes, juice
1 tbsp olive oil
salt
pepper
1 large avocado, diced
8 tostadas

Directions

1. Get a mixing bowl: Stir in it the tuna, onion, tomato, cucumber, and cilantro.
2. Pour over them the lime juice, olive oil, salt, and pepper. Toss them to coat.
3. Stir in the serrano chilies, followed by avocado.
4. Spoon your ceviche into tostadas then serve them right away.
5. Enjoy.

CEVICHE
Micronesia

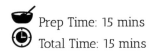 Prep Time: 15 mins

Total Time: 15 mins

Servings per Recipe: 4
Calories   308.3
Fat   14.4g
Cholesterol   51.0mg
Sodium   95.2mg
Carbohydrates   17.5g
Protein   29.9g

Ingredients

1 lb. yellowfin tuna fillet, cubed
3/4 C. lime juice
2 tomatoes, chopped
1/2 small onion, minced
1 cucumber, diced
1 carrot, shredded
1 C. coconut milk

1 green bell pepper, sliced
spring onion
parsley

Directions

1. Get a mixing bowl: Place in it the fish and cover it with seawater or salted water. Let it sit for 10 min.
2. Once the time is up, drain the tuna and transfer it to a mixing bowl.
3. Add to it the lemon juice. Let them sit for 6 min.
4. Once the time is up, discard 2/3 of the lemon juice covering the fish.
5. Add to them the remaining ingredients. Toss them to coat.
6. Adjust the seasoning of your ceviche then serve it.
7. Enjoy.

Mango
Ceviche Wraps

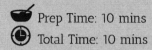 Prep Time: 10 mins

Total Time: 10 mins

Servings per Recipe: 4
Calories	260.8
Fat	14.8g
Cholesterol	18.7mg
Sodium	1221.7mg
Carbohydrates	15.3g
Protein	19.1g

Ingredients

250 g tuna fish, cubed
1 mango, cubed
1 avocado, cubed
Sauce
4 tbsp light soy sauce
4 tbsp lime juice

chili powder
2 tbsp olive oil
2 tbsp balsamic vinegar

Directions

1. Get a mixing bowl: Toss in it all the ingredients.
2. Cover it and chill it in the fridge for 1 h or serve it immediately.
3. Enjoy.

PINEAPPLE
Ceviche with Fried Cinnamon Pastry

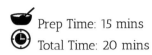 Prep Time: 15 mins

Total Time: 20 mins

Servings per Recipe: 4
Calories	597.8
Fat	35.4g
Cholesterol	0.0mg
Sodium	699.6mg
Carbohydrates	64.7g
Protein	5.5g

Ingredients

Dough
1 (15 oz.) packages Pillsbury pie crusts
cinnamon
honey
vegetable oil
Ceviche
1/4 fresh pineapple, diced
1/4 cantaloupe, diced

1/2 pint strawberry, diced
1/4 C. fresh orange juice
3 tbsp tequila, flamed to remove alcohol ,
optional
3 tbsp agave nectar

Directions

1. Get a mixing bowl: Wisk in it the orange juice, tequila, and nectar.
2. Add the diced fruits and toss them to coat. Chill it in the fridge for at least 3 h.
3. Place a deep skillet over medium-high heat. Heat in it 1 inch of oil.
4. Slice the pie crust into 4 pieces. Fry them in the hot oil until they become golden brown.
5. Drain them and place them on some paper towels to drain.
6. Arrange the golden pie pieces on a serving plate. Top them with some cinnamon and honey.
7. Serve them with the fruit ceviche.
8. Enjoy.

Simple
Ceviche Formulae

🥣 Prep Time: 20 mins
🕐 Total Time: 20 mins

Servings per Recipe: 6
Calories   335.5
Fat   11.2g
Cholesterol   95.5mg
Sodium   859.0mg
Carbohydrates   0.8g
Protein   53.8g

Ingredients

3 lbs. boneless white fish, skinless, cubed
lime juice
orange juice
2 tbsp white vinegar
kosher salt & ground black pepper
2 tbsp olive oil

1/4 small red onion, chopped
3 green onions, trimmed and chopped
1 celery rib, chopped
2 tbsp cilantro, chopped

Directions

1. Get a mixing bowl: Stir in it the fish with the juice of 2 limes.
2. Chill it in the fridge for 16 min.
3. Get a mixing bowl: Whisk in it the juice of 1 lime, orange juice, vinegar, salt, pepper, and olive oil.
4. Drain the fish and add it with onion, green onion, celery, and cilantro. Toss them to coat.
5. Chill the ceviche in the fridge for 3 h then serve it.
6. Enjoy.

WATERCRESS
Salad

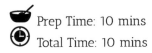 Prep Time: 10 mins

Total Time: 10 mins

Servings per Recipe: 8

Calories	114.5
Fat	10.0g
Cholesterol	0.0mg
Sodium	53.9mg
Carbohydrates	5.4g
Protein	3.4g

Ingredients

18 oz. spinach, fresh
1 bunch watercress
7 scallions, chopped
2 garlic cloves

1 1/2 C. vinaigrette
1 C. Caramelized pecans, or normal pecans

Directions

1. Get a large mixing bowl: Combine in it the watercress with spinach.
2. Drizzle some of the vinaigrette all over it. Sprinkle the caramelized pecans scallions over them. Drizzle more vinaigrette on top.
3. Serve your salad right away.
4. Enjoy.

Provolone Mortadella Sandwiches

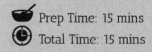

Prep Time: 15 mins
Total Time: 15 mins

Servings per Recipe: 4
Calories	662.6
Fat	62.5g
Cholesterol	61.5mg
Sodium	1805.0mg
Carbohydrates	8.0g
Protein	19.3g

Ingredients

1 roasted red pepper, chopped
4 oz. black olives, chopped
4 oz. green olives, chopped
4 oz. extra virgin olive oil
2 tbsp chopped parsley
2 anchovy fillets, chopped
1 tsp dried oregano
1 tbsp lemon juice
1 1/2 oz. lettuce, shredded
6 oz. chopped tomatoes
6 oz. sliced mortadella
4 oz. sliced jerk sausage
4 oz. provolone cheese, sliced thinly
Pepper
Salt

Directions

1. Get a mixing bowl: Stir in it the red pepper, olives, olive oil, and parsley, anchovies, oregano and lemon juice to make the salad.
2. Slice 4 bread rolls of your choice in half and place them aside.
3. Pour the olives and pepper salad in a colander and drain it then place it aside.
4. Brush the bread rolls with the drained oil. Divide half the olives and pepper salad between them followed by all the greens, tomato, meats and cheese.
5. Lay the remaining salad on top. Cover the sandwiches completely with a plastic wrap and place them in the fridge for 2 h to an overnight.
6. Serve them with your favorite sauce.
7. Enjoy.

NUTMEG
Beef and Plantain Kabobs

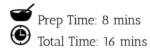

Prep Time: 8 mins
Total Time: 16 mins

Servings per Recipe: 6
Calories	388.6
Fat	17.9g
Cholesterol	102.0mg
Sodium	524.2mg
Carbohydrates	24.5g
Protein	33.3g

Ingredients

1/2 C. chopped green onion
1 tbsp ground allspice
2 tbsp red wine vinegar
1 tsp salt
1 tsp chopped thyme
2 tsp soy sauce
1/2 tsp ground cinnamon
1/8 tsp ground nutmeg
2 habaneros, seeded

1 1/2 lbs boneless sirloin, cubes
1 red bell pepper, chopped
1 red bell pepper, chopped
2 black-ripe plantains, peeled, chunked
cooking spray

Directions

1. Before you do anything, preheat the grill and grease it.
2. Get a food processor: Combine in it the green onions, allspice, vinegar, salt thyme, soy sauce, cinnamon, nutmeg and hot peppers. Blend them smooth.
3. Get a large zip lock bag: Mix in it the beef chunks with bell pepper, and green onion mix. Seal the bag and refrigerate it for 25 min.
4. In the meantime, preheat the grill.
5. Once the time is up, drain the bell pepper, plantain, and beef pieces. Thread them into skewers while alternating between them.
6. Grease the grill and grill in it the kabobs for 5 to 7 min on each side. Serve them right away.
7. Enjoy.

Jerk Flounder
Fillets with Mango Sauce

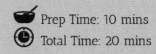 Prep Time: 10 mins

Total Time: 20 mins

Servings per Recipe: 4
Calories	467.8
Fat	22.3g
Cholesterol	92.2mg
Sodium	459.3mg
Carbohydrates	34.8g
Protein	33.5g

Ingredients

4 flounder fillets
3 tbsp jamaican jerk rub
2 tbsp vegetable oil
1/2 C. whole wheat flour
2/3 C. mayonnaise

4 limes
4 tbsp mango preserves
8 -10 fresh basil leaves

Directions

1. Place a large pan over medium heat. Heat the oil in it.
2. Season the flounder fillets with some salt and pepper. Coat them with jerk rub. Dust them lightly in the flour and fry them in the hot oil for 6 min on each side.
3. Get a small mixing bowl: Combine in it the mango preserves and mayo in a mixing bowl.
4. Add the grazed zest of the 3 limes and the juice of 4 limes. Stir them well.
5. Serve your fried jerk flounder with the mango salsa.
6. Enjoy.

NUTTY
Pineapple Rice Pudding

 Prep Time: 15 mins

Total Time: 20 mins

Servings per Recipe: 4

Calories	304.0
Fat	8.8g
Cholesterol	0.0mg
Sodium	15.8m
Carbohydrates	52.5g
Protein	6.4g

Ingredients

2 C. cooked rice
1 cans oranges, chopped
1 cans pineapple, drained
1/2 C. chopped red bell pepper
1/2 C. almonds, toasted
1/3 C. sliced green onion
1/4 C. flaked coconut, toasted

2 tbsp mango chutney
1/4 tsp ground ginger

Directions

1. Place a large pan over medium heat. Stir in it all the ingredients. Cook them for 6 min while stirring them all the time.
2. Serve your pudding warm with your favorite toppings.
3. Enjoy.

Jerk
Shrimp Soup

🥣 Prep Time: 5 mins
🕐 Total Time: 15 mins

Servings per Recipe: 4
Calories	108.7
Fat	3.3g
Cholesterol	67.8mg
Sodium	140.2mg
Carbohydrates	10.0g
Protein	9.9g

Ingredients

2 tsp oil
1 bunch scallion, chopped
1 (7 ounce) cans sweetcorn, drained
1 stalk celery, sliced
1 tsp jamaican jerk spice

6 oz. large shrimp, defrosted
2 tbsp cornstarch
1 3/4 pints vegetable stock

Directions

1. Place a pot over medium heat. Heat the oil in it. Add the celery with corn and scallions. Cook them for 3 min.

2. Stir in the shrimp with the jerk seasoning.

3. Get a mixing bowl: Whisk in it the stock with cornstarch. Pour the mix all over the shrimp, cook it until it starts boiling.

4. Let the soup cook for an extra 3 to 4 min. Serve it warm.

5. Enjoy.

KABOBS
Kingston

Prep Time: 5 mins
Total Time: 20 mins

Servings per Recipe: 4
Calories   474.2
Fat   33.6g
Cholesterol   109.3mg
Sodium   634.4mg
Carbohydrates   10.5g
Protein   32.2g

Ingredients

1/4 C. olive oil
1 lime, juiced
2 garlic cloves, minced
2 tbsp minced fresh oregano
1 tbsp lime peel, grated
1 tbsp onion powder
1 tbsp light brown sugar
1/2 tsp ground allspice
1/4 tsp ground cinnamon

1/4 tsp cayenne pepper
Kabobs:
1 lb boneless skinless chicken breast, diced
8 oz. light smoked sausage, diced
2 green bell peppers, cut into 1 inch pieces

Directions

1. Before you do anything, preheat the grill and grease it.
2. Get a mixing bowl: Whisk in it the olive oil, lime juice, garlic, oregano, lime peel, onion powder, brown sugar, allspice, cinnamon, and cayenne.
3. Thread the bell pepper with chicken and sausages into skewers while alternating between them.
4. Cook the kabobs for 8 to 9 min on each side while coating them with the glaze every 2 or 3 min.
5. Serve your kabobs warm.
6. Enjoy.

Tropical
Seafood Skillet

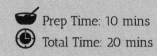

Prep Time: 10 mins
Total Time: 20 mins

Servings per Recipe: 4
Calories	260.5
Fat	12.3g
Cholesterol	205.3mg
Sodium	368.3mg
Carbohydrates	8.3g
Protein	28.7g

Ingredients

2 tbsp butter
1/2 medium onion, chopped
1/2 green pepper, chopped
4 large white fish fillets, cut into chunks
200 g small shrimp, chopped
75 g coconut cream, grated
1/2-1 tbsp scotch bonnet chili sauce
1 large egg yolk, mixed with 1 tbsp cornstarch
4 tbsp chopped coriander

1/4 tsp salt
1/4 tsp pepper
1 lime, to serve

Directions

1. Place a deep skillet over medium heat. Melt the butter in it. Add the onion and cook it for 4 min.
2. Stir the coconut cream until it melts. Pour all over it the fish, prawns, chili sauce and 1/2 C. of water. Stir them well.
3. Let them cook for 6 min. stir the egg yolk mixture to the skillet with a pinch of salt and pepper. Let them cook for few minutes until the sauce becomes thick.
4. Serve your creamy shrimp and fish skillet warm with some rice or noodles.
5. Enjoy.

NEW AGE
Lemonade

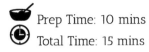 Prep Time: 10 mins

Total Time: 15 mins

Servings per Recipe: 8
Calories   124.8
Fat   0.0g
Cholesterol   0.0mg
Sodium   4.5mg0
Carbohydrates   32.7g
Protein   0.4g

Ingredients

1 C. sugar
1 C. boiling water
3 1/2 C. cold water, divided

3 C. peeled chopped papayas
1 C. fresh lemon juice

Directions

1. In a bowl, add the sugar and boiling water and stir till sugar is dissolved.
2. Keep aside to cool slightly.
3. In a blender, add the sugar syrup, 2 C. of the cold water, papaya and lemon juice and pulse till smooth.
4. Stir in the remaining 1 1/2 C. of the cold water.
5. Serve over the ice.

Shrimp and Fruit Lunch Wraps

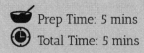 Prep Time: 5 mins
Total Time: 5 mins

Servings per Recipe: 6
Calories	69.9
Fat	0.8g
Cholesterol	79.7mg
Sodium	424.1mg
Carbohydrates	6.5g
Protein	9.4g

Ingredients

1/3 C. lime juice
1 tsp balsamic vinegar
1/4 C. chopped fresh Thai basil
1/4 C. chopped green onion
2 cloves garlic, finely minced
1 pickled jalapeno pepper, minced
1/2 tsp brown sugar

1 small papaya, peeled and cubed
1/2 lb cooked and shelled small baby shrimp
fish sauce, to taste
24 butter lettuce leaves

Directions

1. In a non-reactive bowl, mix together the lime juice, balsamic vinegar, basil, green onion, garlic, jalapeño and brown sugar.
2. Stir in the cubed papaya, shrimp and fish sauce.
3. In a shallow dish, place the shrimp mixture and arrange the butter lettuce leaves around it.
4. Use the lettuce leaves to scoop up the papaya mixture and hold to eat

SWEETENED
Condensed
Milkshake

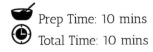

Prep Time: 10 mins
Total Time: 10 mins

Servings per Recipe: 6
Calories	69.9
Fat	0.8g
Cholesterol	79.7mg
Sodium	424.1mg
Carbohydrates	6.5g
Protein	9.4g

Ingredients

1 medium ripe papaya, peeled, seeded
and chopped roughly
1 C. evaporated milk
3 oz. sweetened condensed milk

1/2 tsp cinnamon
2 C. finely crushed ice

Directions

1. In a blender, add the papaya, milk, cinnamon and ice and pulse on high speed till smooth.

Southern
Papaya Starter

Prep Time: 15 mins
Total Time: 15 mins

Servings per Recipe: 12

Calories	96.4
Fat	3.4g
Cholesterol	7.6mg
Sodium	136.3mg5
Carbohydrates	14.8g
Protein	1.8g

Ingredients

1 papaya, peeled and seeded
3 tbsp butter
1/2 loaf French bread, sliced into 12 slices
(the skinny baguette)
1 lemon, juice of

2 tbsp sugar
1/2 tsp ground cinnamon
of fresh mint, for garnish

Directions

1. Slice the papaya into thin rounds.
2. In a small bowl, mix together the sugar and cinnamon.
3. Butter the bread slices lightly and top with a thin round of papaya.
4. Sprinkle with the cinnamon sugar and cover with another thin slice of papaya.
5. Lightly, drizzle with the lemon juice.
6. Serve with a garnishing of the mint leaves.

SANIBEL ISLAND
Parfaits

Prep Time: 15 mins
Total Time: 15 mins

Servings per Recipe: 6
Calories	256.9
Fat	5.6g
Cholesterol	0.0mg
Sodium	25.1mg1
Carbohydrates	54.7g
Protein	2.9g

Ingredients

1/2 large fresh pineapple, peeled cored cubed
2 papayas, peeled seeded cubed
1 mango, peeled pitted chopped
1 banana

1/2 C. freshly squeezed orange juice
1/2 C. grated coconut

Directions

1. In a large bowl, mix together the pineapple, papaya and mango.
2. In a food processor, add the banana and orange juice and pulse till smooth.
3. Fill the tall dessert glasses with the fruit halfway and top with the banana mixture, stirring just to
4. Mix with a plastic wrap, cover the glasses and refrigerate to chill for several hours.
5. Serve with a sprinkling of the grated coconut.

Peach
and Papaya Sorbet

Prep Time: 3 mins
Total Time: 5 mins

Servings per Recipe: 6
Calories   256.9
Fat   5.6g
Cholesterol   0.0mg
Sodium   25.1mg1
Carbohydrates   54.7g
Protein   2.9g

Ingredients

1 medium banana
1 C. papaya, chunks
1 C. peach, chunks

2 tbsp water
1 tbsp lemon juice

Directions

1. On a wax paper-lined rimmed baking sheet arrange the fruit slices and freeze for about 1 1/2-2 hours.
2. In a food processor, add the fruit, water and lemon juice and pulse till smooth.
3. Serve immediately.

BANGKOK
Curry Stir Fry

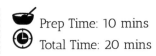

Prep Time: 10 mins
Total Time: 20 mins

Servings per Recipe: 4

Calories	271 kcal
Fat	15.8 g
Carbohydrates	11.2g
Protein	25.4 g
Cholesterol	59 mg
Sodium	147 mg

Ingredients

2 tsp olive oil
1 lb skinless, boneless chicken breast
halves - cut into thin strips
1 tbsp Thai red curry paste
1 C. sliced halved zucchini
1 red bell pepper, seeded and sliced into
strips
1/2 C. sliced carrots
1 onion, quartered then halved

1 tbsp cornstarch
1 (14 oz) can light coconut milk
2 tbsp chopped fresh cilantro

Directions

1. Place a large pan over medium heat. Heat the oil in it. Cook in it the chicken for 4 min.
2. Stir in the curry paste, zucchini, bell pepper, carrot and onion then cook them for 4 min.
3. Get a small mixing bowl: Whisk in it the cornstarch with coconut milk. Stir the mix into the skillet. Cook the stir fry until it starts boiling.
4. Lower the heat and cook the stir fry for 2 min. Serve it warm.
5. Enjoy.

Nutty Chicken and Carrot Stir Fry

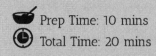

Prep Time: 10 mins

Total Time: 20 mins

Servings per Recipe: 6	
Calories	235 kcal
Fat	7.9 g
Carbohydrates	12.9 g
Protein	27.4 g
Cholesterol	69 mg
Sodium	529 mg

Ingredients

2 tsp peanut oil
2 stalks celery, chopped
2 carrots, peeled and diagonally sliced
1 1/2 lb skinless, boneless chicken breast
halves - cut into strips
1 tbsp cornstarch
3/4 C. orange juice

3 tbsp light soy sauce
1 tbsp honey
1 tsp minced fresh ginger root
1/4 C. cashews
1/4 C. minced green onions

Directions

1. Place a large skillet over medium heat. Heat 1 teaspoon of oil in it.
2. Cook in it the celery with carrot for 4 min. Stir in the remaining oil with chicken then cook them for 6 min.
3. Get a small mixing bowl: Whisk in it the orange juice with cornstarch. Add the soy sauce, honey and ginger then whisk them to make the sauce.
4. Stir the sauce to the pan and cook them until the sauce becomes thick. Serve your chicken stir fry warm with some cashews and green onions.
5. Enjoy.

COOKOUT
Bananas

Prep Time: 5 mins
Total Time: 15 mins

Servings per Recipe: 4
Calories	148 kcal
Fat	0.5 g
Carbohydrates	38.1g
Protein	1.5 g
Cholesterol	0 mg
Sodium	3 mg

Ingredients

4 banana, peeled and halved lengthwise
1 tablespoon brown sugar
2 teaspoons lemon juice

2 teaspoons honey
splash of orange juice

Directions

1. Cover a casserole dish with foil then set your oven to 450 degrees before doing anything else.
2. Layer you banana on the dish then top them with the orange juice, brown sugar, honey, and lemon juice.
3. Place a covering of foil on the dish and cook everything in the oven for 7 mins.
4. Enjoy.

Yellow Jacket
Crepes

Prep Time: 5 mins
Total Time: 20 mins

Servings per Recipe: 6
Calories	518 kcal
Fat	28.7 g
Carbohydrates	60.7g
Protein	8 g
Cholesterol	146 mg
Sodium	252 mg

Ingredients

1 cup all-purpose flour
1/4 cup confectioners' sugar
2 eggs
1 cup milk
3 tablespoons butter, melted
1 teaspoon vanilla extract
1/4 teaspoon salt
1/4 cup butter

1/4 cup packed brown sugar
1/4 teaspoon ground cinnamon
1/4 teaspoon ground nutmeg
1/4 cup half-and-half cream
6 bananas, halved lengthwise
1 1/2 cups whipped heavy cream
1 pinch ground cinnamon

Directions

1. Get a bowl and sift in your powdered sugar and flour. Combine in the salt, eggs, butter, and milk and work the mix completely.

2. Get a frying pan hot with some oil then ladle in about 3 tbsps of the mix and spread the mix to form a nice sized crepe.

3. Let the crepe cook until the bottom is slightly brown for about 3 mins then flip it and cook it the opposite for the same amount of time.

4. When you start another crepe add a bit more oil or butter to the pan.

5. Once all the crepes have been cooked add 1/4 cup of butter to a small pot and get it melted.

6. Combine in 1/4 tsp of cinnamon and nutmeg then add in the brown sugar as well.

7. Stir the mix then stir in the cream and heat everything until it is slightly thick.

8. Begin to fry half of the bananas in the crepe frying pan for 4 mins then top them with the sauce.

9. Place some banana on each crepe then serve it with a topping of more sauce, cinnamon, and whipped cream.

10. Enjoy.

SKILLET
Buttery Bananas

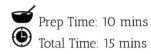 Prep Time: 10 mins

Total Time: 15 mins

Servings per Recipe: 6

Calories	169 kcal
Fat	6 g
Carbohydrates	30.5g
Protein	0.7 g
Cholesterol	15 mg
Sodium	42 mg

Ingredients

3 firm bananas, halved lengthwise
1/2 cup white sugar
1 1/4 teaspoons ground cinnamon

3 tablespoons butter

Directions

1. Slice your banana into two pieces, then cut each half into 4 additional pieces.
2. Get a bowl combine: cinnamon and sugar.
3. Get your butter hot in a frying pan then layer in the banana and fry them for 7 mins.
4. Flip the bananas half way.
5. When serving the bananas coat them with some of the sugar mix.
6. Enjoy

Colada
Skillet Bananas

Prep Time: 5 mins
Total Time: 15 mins

Servings per Recipe: 6
Calories	405 kcal
Fat	19.5 g
Carbohydrates	48.6 g
Protein	5.5 g
Cholesterol	23 mg
Sodium	23 mg

Ingredients

1/2 cup semi-sweet chocolate chips
1/3 cup whipping cream
1/2 teaspoon vanilla extract
1/2 cup pina colada soda

1 tablespoon butter
6 bananas, peeled and halved lengthwise
1 cup toasted sliced almonds

Directions

1. Melt and stir the following in a pot: vanilla extract, chocolate and cream.
2. Once the chocolate is completely melted add in the soda and shut the heat.
3. Get your butter hot and melted in a frying pan then combine in the banana and fry them for 4 mins each side.
4. Divide your bananas into servings on plates then top them evenly with the sauce and some almonds.
5. Enjoy.

FRESH SPINACH, Mango, and Coconut Smoothie

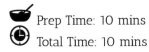 Prep Time: 10 mins

Total Time: 10 mins

Servings per Recipe: 2

Calories	374 kcal
Fat	25.6 g
Carbohydrates	37g
Protein	6.3 g
Cholesterol	0 mg
Sodium	116 mg

Ingredients

Smoothie:
3 C. fresh spinach
1 banana
1/2 (14 oz.) can coconut milk
1/2 C. frozen mango chunks
1/2 C. coconut water
Toppings:
1/3 C. fresh raspberries

1/4 C. fresh blueberries
2 tbsps granola
1 tbsp coconut flakes
1/4 tsp sliced almonds
1/4 tsp chia seeds (optional)

Directions

1. Add the following to a food processor: coconut water, spinach, mango, coconut milk, and banana. Puree the mix until it smooth then put everything into a larger bowl. Top the mix with your chia, raspberries, almonds, blue berries, and coconut flakes.

2. Stir everything again.

3. Enjoy.

Greek Yogurt and Granola Bowl

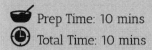 Prep Time: 10 mins
Total Time: 10 mins

Servings per Recipe: 2

Calories	394 kcal
Fat	16.8 g
Carbohydrates	54.4g
Protein	11.2 g
Cholesterol	22 mg
Sodium	138 mg

Ingredients

Smoothie:
1 C. frozen strawberries
1 C. frozen pineapple chunks
1 C. plain Greek yogurt
1/2 C. coconut water
2 tbsps frozen acai berry pulp, or as desired
Toppings:
1 kiwi, peeled and sliced

1/2 banana, sliced
1/2 C. fresh blueberries
1/2 C. fresh raspberries
2 tbsps sliced almonds
2 tbsps granola
1 tsp chia seeds (optional)

Directions

1. Add the following to your food processor and puree it: acai, strawberries, coconut water, yogurt, and pineapple. Enter everything into a bowl, and top the mix with your chia, kiwi, granola, banana, almonds, raspberries, and blueberries.

2. Enjoy

CUTE
Sorbet

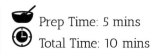 Prep Time: 5 mins
Total Time: 10 mins

Servings per Recipe: 2
Calories   183 kcal
Fat   0.1 g
Carbohydrates   44.8g
Protein   0.2 g
Cholesterol   0 mg
Sodium   18 mg

Ingredients

1 C. vanilla, strawberry or raspberry
sorbet, frozen yogurt or ice cream,
softened
1 (8.4 oz.) can Juice Drink, any flavor,
chilled

Fresh strawberry slices or raspberries,
garnish

Directions

1. Separate the sorbet into serving bowls then stir each one to make it softer.
2. Add in the juice and stir everything again then top each one with some berries.
3. Enjoy.

Easy
English Sorbet

Prep Time: 10 mins
Total Time: 10 mins

Servings per Recipe: 4
Calories   175 kcal
Fat   0.3 g
Carbohydrates   45.9g
Protein   0.9 g
Cholesterol   0 mg
Sodium   4 mg

Ingredients

1 fresh pineapple - peeled, cored and cut into chunks
2 large green apples, washed and sliced
1 1/4 tsps chopped fresh ginger

1 C. brewed green tea, chilled
1 C. mango sorbet or crushed ice

Directions

1. Add your ginger, apples, and pineapples into a juicer.
2. Add the tea to the juice then stir everything completely then add in the sorbet and stir the again until it is evenly combined.
3. Enjoy.

MID-SUMMER
Night Salad

Prep Time: 20 mins
Total Time: 20 mins

Servings per Recipe: 6
Calories	189 kcal
Fat	7.6 g
Carbohydrates	24.7g
Protein	6.9 g
Cholesterol	0 mg
Sodium	607 mg

Ingredients

2 tbsp finely chopped fresh cilantro
2 tbsp fresh lime juice
1 lime, zested
3 tbsp olive oil
1 tsp freshly cracked black pepper
1/2 tsp salt
1 (15 oz.) can black beans, rinsed and drained

1 (15 oz.) can garbanzo beans, rinsed and drained
1/2 tomato, seeded and chopped
1/2 cucumber, seeded and chopped
1/4 red onion, chopped

Directions

1. In a bowl, add the cilantro, lime zest, lime juice, olive oil, salt and black pepper and beat till well combined.
2. In a large bowl, mix together the garbanzo beans, black beans, cucumber, tomato and red onion.
3. Pour the dressing over salad and toss to coat well.
4. Serve Immediately.

Bean Salad Festival

🥄 Prep Time: 15 mins
🕐 Total Time: 15 mins

Servings per Recipe: 4
Calories   274 kcal
Fat   11 g
Carbohydrates   38.7g
Protein   8.7 g
Cholesterol   0 mg
Sodium   419 mg

Ingredients

1 seedless cucumber, quartered and cut into chunks
1 (15 oz.) can black beans, rinsed and drained
1 C. cherry tomatoes, halved
1 C. frozen corn, thawed
1/2 red onion, chopped
3 tbsp extra-virgin olive oil

4 1/2 tsp orange marmalade
1 tbsp lemon juice
1 tsp honey
1/2 tsp ground cumin
salt and ground black pepper to taste

Directions

1. In a large bowl, mix together the black beans, corn, cucumber, tomatoes and onion.
2. In another bowl, add the lemon juice, olive oil, orange marmalade, honey, cumin, salt and black pepper and beat till well combined.
3. Pour the dressing over the cucumber mixture and toss to coat well.
4. Serve immediately.

COLLEGE BEAN
Salad

Prep Time: 15 mins
Total Time: 15 mins

Servings per Recipe: 2
Calories	274 kcal
Fat	7.7 g
Carbohydrates	41.2g
Protein	10.8 g
Cholesterol	0 mg
Sodium	3043 mg

Ingredients

1 (14.5 oz.) can fava beans, drained and rinsed
1/2 onion, chopped (optional)
1/2 tomato, chopped (optional)
1 large lemon, juiced

3 tbsp chopped fresh parsley
1 tbsp extra-virgin olive oil
1 tbsp sea salt (optional)
1 clove garlic, minced

Directions

1. In a large bowl, add all the ingredients and toss to coat well.
2. Serve immediately.

Bean Salad
from the Orient

🥣 Prep Time: 15 mins
🕐 Total Time: 15 mins

Servings per Recipe: 6
Calories   197 kcal
Fat   10.2 g
Carbohydrates   21.9g
Protein   5.5 g
Cholesterol   0 mg
Sodium   299 mg

Ingredients

1/4 C. extra-virgin olive oil
3 tbsp freshly squeezed lemon juice
1 1/2 tsp minced garlic
sea salt to taste
freshly ground black pepper to taste
1 bunch flat-leaf parsley, chopped
1 (15 oz.) can light red kidney beans, drained and rinsed

1 (15 oz.) can garbanzo beans, drained and rinsed
1 C. minced red onion
1 pinch ground sumac (optional)

Directions

1. In a large bowl, add the lemon juice, oil, garlic, salt and black pepper and beat till well combined.
2. Add the remaining ingredients and toss to coat well.

BEANS
& Guacamole Salad

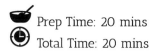
Prep Time: 20 mins
Total Time: 20 mins

Servings per Recipe: 8
Calories   271 kcal
Fat   10.2 g
Carbohydrates   38.9 g
Protein   8.3 g
Cholesterol   3 mg
Sodium   425 mg

Ingredients

1 (15 oz.) can kidney beans, drained
1 (15 oz.) can garbanzo beans, drained
1 C. chopped tomatoes
3/4 C. cucumber - peeled, seeded, and chopped
2 tbsp diced onion
1 (6 oz.) container guacamole
1/2 C. plain yogurt

1/4 tsp salt
1/4 C. milk
shredded lettuce
corn tortilla chips

Directions

1. In a large bowl, mix together the garbanzo beans, kidney beans, cucumber, tomatoes and onion.
2. In a small bowl, add the yogurt, guacamole and salt and mix well.
3. Place the dressing over the beans mixture and stir to combine.
4. Refrigerate to chill before serving.
5. Serve with a topping of the shredded lettuce and corn chips.

Sweet Tuna
Bean Salad

Prep Time: 15 mins
Total Time: 15 mins

Servings per Recipe: 8
Calories	171 kcal
Fat	11.2 g
Carbohydrates	10.9g
Protein	6.4 g
Cholesterol	10 mg
Sodium	593 mg

Ingredients

1 (5 oz.) can tuna, drained and flaked
1/2 red bell pepper
1/2 onion, chopped
3 tbsp chopped fresh cilantro
2 tbsp capers
1/4 C. pickle relish
1/2 C. mayonnaise
1/2 C. Dijon-style mustard

1 tsp garlic powder
1/2 (15 oz.) can white beans, drained
2 tbsp chopped fresh parsley, for garnish

Directions

1. In a food processor, add the tuna, bell pepper, onion, cilantro, capers, mayonnaise, relish, mustard and garlic powder and pulse till smooth.
2. Transfer the tuna mixture into a large bowl with white beans and stir to combine well.
3. Serve with a garnishing of the parsley.

BEAN SALAD
Martinique

Prep Time: 10 mins
Total Time: 12 mins

Servings per Recipe: 4
Calories	72 kcal
Fat	4.4 g
Carbohydrates	8.3g
Protein	1.1 g
Cholesterol	0 mg
Sodium	140 mg

Ingredients

2 C. grated carrots
1/2 C. bean sprouts
1 tsp white sugar
1 tbsp lemon juice
1 tbsp grated fresh coconut

1 tbsp finely chopped cilantro
1 tbsp sunflower seed oil
1 tsp mustard seed
salt to taste

Directions

1. In a large bowl, add the bean sprouts, carrots, cilantro, coconut, sugar and lemon juice and gently, toss to coat.
2. In a small pan, heat the oil on medium heat and sauté the mustard seeds till golden brown.
3. Add the oil mixture into the salad with the salt and stir to combine.
4. Serve immediately.

Green Mango
Salad

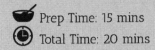

Prep Time: 15 mins
Total Time: 20 mins

Servings per Recipe: 6
Calories	91 kcal
Fat	0.4 g
Carbohydrates	18.3g
Protein	4.8 g
Cholesterol	0 mg
Sodium	339 mg

Ingredients

1 (15 oz.) can black beans, drained and rinsed
1 tsp ground cumin
1 tsp water
1 mango, peeled and diced
1 cucumber, seeded and diced

1 jalapeño pepper, seeded and diced
2 tbsp chopped cilantro
1/2 lime, juiced
salt and ground black pepper to taste

Directions

1. In a microwave-safe bowl, add the black beans, cumin and water and microwave on High for about 1 minute.
2. In a bowl, mix together the mango, cucumber, cilantro, jalapeño pepper, lime juice, salt and black pepper.
3. Stir in the black beans and serve immediately.

PEPPERY
Bean Salad

Prep Time: 10 mins
Total Time: 20 mins

Servings per Recipe: 4
Calories	199 kcal
Fat	7.5 g
Carbohydrates	26.1g
Protein	9.4 g
Cholesterol	0 mg
Sodium	1226 mg

Ingredients

2 tbsp extra-virgin olive oil
1 onion, thinly sliced
1 tsp kosher salt
1/2 tsp red pepper flakes
1/2 tsp ground black pepper
2 cloves garlic, chopped

1 (15 oz.) can black beans, drained
1 (10 oz.) can diced tomatoes with green chile peppers
1 (10 oz.) bag fresh baby spinach

Directions

1. In a large skillet, heat the oil on medium-high heat and cook the onion with salt for about 10-15 minutes.
2. Stir in the garlic, red pepper and black pepper and cook for about 1 minute.
3. Stir in the black beans and tomatoes and cook for about 5 minutes.
4. Remove from the heat and stir in the spinach.
5. Keep aside, covered for about 3 minutes.
6. Toss the mixture well and serve.

Italian
Cannellini Salad

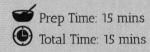 Prep Time: 15 mins
Total Time: 15 mins

Servings per Recipe: 8
Calories	193 kcal
Fat	7.6 g
Carbohydrates	24.9g
Protein	6.8 g
Cholesterol	0 mg
Sodium	328 mg

Ingredients

1 (15 oz.) can cannellini (white kidney) beans, rinsed and drained
1 (15 oz.) can garbanzo beans, rinsed and drained
1 (15 oz.) can dark red kidney beans, rinsed and drained
1/2 onion, minced

2 cloves garlic, minced
2 tbsp minced fresh parsley
1/4 C. olive oil
1 lemon, juiced
salt and ground black pepper to taste

Directions

1. In a large bowl, add all the ingredients and mix till well combined.
2. Serve immediately.

QUICK
Dumplings

Prep Time: 10 mins
Total Time: 10 mins

Servings per Recipe: 6
Calories	173 kcal
Fat	1.2 g
Carbohydrates	34.1g
Protein	5.6 g
Cholesterol	3 mg
Sodium	568 mg

Ingredients

2 C. all-purpose flour
2 tsp baking powder
1 tsp salt

1 C. milk

Directions

1. Get a large mixing bowl: Stir in it the flour with baking powder and a pinch of salt. Add the mix gradually while whisking all the time until the dough becomes soft.
2. Cook the dumplings the way you desire.
3. Enjoy.

Italian
Herbs Dumplings

Prep Time: 5 mins
Total Time: 20 mins

Servings per Recipe: 6
Calories	182 kcal
Fat	6.7 g
Carbohydrates	25.9 g
Protein	4.4 g
Cholesterol	18 mg
Sodium	772 mg

Ingredients

1 1/2 C. all-purpose flour
1 tsp salt
1 tsp baking soda
2 tsp baking powder
1 tsp dried thyme
1 tsp dried parsley

1 tsp dried oregano
3 tbsp butter
3/4 C. milk

Directions

1. Get a large mixing bowl: Stir in it the flour, salt, baking soda, baking powder, thyme, parsley, and oregano. Add the butter and mix them until they become crumbled.
2. Drizzle the milk gradually while mixing all the time until you get a smooth dough.
3. Spoon the dumplings and drop them on your soup, stew or broth. Put on the lid and cook them for 17 min. Serve them warm.
4. Enjoy.

SPICY FRUIT
and Chicken Salad

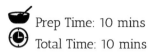

Prep Time: 10 mins
Total Time: 10 mins

Servings per Recipe: 8	
Calories	306 kcal
Fat	23 g
Carbohydrates	11.5g
Protein	15 g
Cholesterol	44 mg
Sodium	153 mg

Ingredients

4 skinless, boneless chicken breast
halves - cooked and diced
1 stalk celery, chopped
1/2 onion, chopped
1 small apple - peeled, cored and
chopped
1/3 C. golden raisins
1/3 C. seedless green grapes, halved

1/2 C. chopped toasted pecans
1/8 tsp ground black pepper
1/2 tsp curry powder
3/4 C. mayonnaise

Directions

1. Get a bowl, mix: mayo, chicken, curry, celery, pepper, onion, pecans, apple, grapes, and
   raisins. Mix everything evenly.
2. Enjoy.

4-Ingredient
Fruit Salad

Prep Time: 10 mins
Total Time: 10 mins

Servings per Recipe: 12
Calories	81 kcal
Fat	0.6 g
Carbohydrates	< 19.2g
Protein	1.5 g
Cholesterol	2 mg
Sodium	< 11 mg

Ingredients

1 pint fresh strawberries, sliced
1 pound seedless green grapes, halved
3 bananas, peeled and sliced

1 8 oz. container strawberry yogurt

Directions

1. Get a salad bowl, combine: yogurt, strawberries, bananas, and grapes.
2. Enjoy.

COUNTRY
Honey Pine Nut Salad

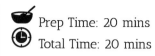
Prep Time: 20 mins
Total Time: 20 mins

Servings per Recipe: 8
Calories   115 kcal
Fat   3.3 g
Carbohydrates   22.3g
Protein   2.4 g
Cholesterol   0 mg
Sodium   2 mg

Ingredients

2 large bananas, sliced
1 16 oz. package fresh strawberries,
hulled and sliced
1/2 pound fresh blueberries

2 tbsps honey
1 lime, juiced
1/3 C. pine nuts

Directions

1. Get a bowl, mix: blueberries, bananas, and strawberries. Toss everything evenly then add your lime and toss again then add the honey and toss again. Finally garnish the salad with the pine nuts and place a covering of plastic on the bowl.

2. Chill the salad in the fridge.

3. Enjoy.

Joey's
Fruit Salad

🥣 Prep Time: 5 mins

🕐 Total Time: 5 mins

Servings per Recipe: 6

Calories	104 kcal
Fat	0.3 g
Carbohydrates	< 26.8g
Protein	1 g
Cholesterol	0 mg
Sodium	2 mg

Ingredients

1 15 oz. can pineapple chunks with juice
1 apple - peeled, cored and diced
1 orange - peeled, diced and juice reserved
1 banana, sliced

1 C. seedless green grapes, halved

Directions

1. Get a bowl, combine: grapes, pineapple, banana, orange, and apple.
2. Toss the salad together then combine in the orange and pineapple juice and toss everything again.
3. Enjoy.

PORT KINGSTON
Style Salad

Prep Time: 15 mins
Total Time: 15 mins

Servings per Recipe: 6
Calories	280 kcal
Fat	12.8 g
Carbohydrates	33g
Protein	11 g
Cholesterol	17 mg
Sodium	357 mg

Ingredients

2 mangos - peeled, seeded, and diced
1 C. reduced fat raspberry vinaigrette
salad dressing
8 C. mixed torn salad greens
1/4 C. chopped cilantro
1/4 C. sliced red onion
1/2 C. fresh raspberries
1/2 C. fresh blackberries

1/2 C. fresh strawberries, halved
1/2 C. fresh blueberries
1/2 C. toasted hazelnuts
4 oz. freshly grated Parmesan cheese

Directions

1. Get your food processor and add in the vinaigrette and 1 diced mango. Puree the mix completely.
2. Get a bowl, combine: onion, the rest of the mango, cilantro, and salad greens. Toss the mix evenly then combine the fruit with the dressing.
3. Add in the berries and toss everything again then garnish each serving of salad with an equal part of parmesan.
4. Enjoy.

Apple
and Yogurt Salad

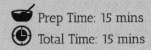 Prep Time: 15 mins
Total Time: 15 mins

Servings per Recipe: 6

Calories	229 kcal
Fat	13.8 g
Carbohydrates	24.9 g
Protein	5.8 g
Cholesterol	2 mg
Sodium	< 28 mg

Ingredients

2 C. diced apples
1 C. sliced banana
1 C. sliced fresh strawberries
1 C. chopped walnuts

1 C. vanilla yogurt
3/4 tsp ground cinnamon

Directions

1. Get a bowl, combine: walnuts, apples, strawberries, and banana. Toss everything evenly then combine in the yogurt and toss everything again. Garnish the salad with your cinnamon and mix everything evenly.

2. Enjoy.

DATES
and Walnut Salad

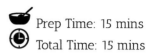

Prep Time: 15 mins
Total Time: 15 mins

Servings per Recipe: 4
Calories	187 kcal
Fat	5.5 g
Carbohydrates	36.1g
Protein	3 g
Cholesterol	0 mg
Sodium	2 mg

Ingredients

2 oranges, peeled and cut into bite size
pieces
1 C. seedless red grapes
1/2 C. pitted and halved Bing cherries
1/4 C. golden raisins

1/4 C. chopped pitted dates
1/4 C. walnut halves

Directions

1. Get a salad bowl, combine: orange, walnuts, grapes, dates, cherries, and raisins. Toss everything completely then place a covering of plastic on the bowl and put the salad in the freezer until it is chilled.
2. Enjoy.

Wednesday's
Lunch Salad

Prep Time: 20 mins
Total Time: 20 mins

Servings per Recipe: 6
Calories	246 kcal
Fat	22.9 g
Carbohydrates	10g
Protein	3.1 g
Cholesterol	0 mg
Sodium	231 mg

Ingredients

Dressing:
1/2 C. vegetable oil
1/4 C. lemon juice
2 tbsps spicy brown mustard
1 tsp white sugar
1/2 tsp kosher salt
1/4 tsp ground white pepper
1 pinch ground black pepper
Salad:
1 head romaine lettuce, torn into bite-size pieces

1/2 small red onion
1/2 C. fresh blueberries
1/2 C. sliced toasted almonds
1 3 oz. can mandarin oranges, drained
4 strawberries, sliced or more to taste

Directions

1. Get a bowl, combine: black pepper, oil, white pepper, mustard, lemon juice, sugar, and salt.
2. Get a 2nd bowl, combine: strawberries, lettuce, mandarin, onion, almonds, and blueberries.
3. Combine both bowls and toss the salad evenly.
4. Enjoy.

HOTEL LOBBY
Cocktail and Banana Salad

Prep Time: 15 mins
Total Time: 15 mins

Servings per Recipe: 12

Calories	202 kcal
Fat	7.5 g
Carbohydrates	34.6g
Protein	1.1 g
Cholesterol	27 mg
Sodium	12 mg

Ingredients

2 15.25 oz. cans fruit cocktail, drained
3 large bananas, peeled and sliced
1 10 oz. jar maraschino cherries, halved
1/2 pint heavy whipping cream

3 tbsps white sugar
1 tsp vanilla extract

Directions

1. Get a bowl, combine: cherries, bananas, and fruit cocktail.
2. Get a 2nd bowl for the heavy cream and with a mixer begin to beat the mix, until peaking then combine in the vanilla and sugar and continue to beat the cream.
3. Combine both bowls and toss the salad.
4. Enjoy.

A 3rd Grader's
Lunch

🥣 Prep Time: 15 mins
🕐 Total Time: 15 mins

Servings per Recipe: 2
Calories	300 kcal
Fat	2.2 g
Carbohydrates	61.5g
Protein	9.9 g
Cholesterol	22 mg
Sodium	129 mg

Ingredients

1/4 fresh pineapple, cut into bite-size chunks
1 orange, peeled and cut into bite-size pieces
1/2 red apple, cut into bite-size pieces
5 seedless red grapes, halved

5 seedless green grapes, halved
2 C. Greek yogurt

Directions

1. Get a bowl, combine: green grapes, pineapple, red grapes, apple, and orange. Toss the salad lightly then top it with the yogurt and stir everything once.
2. Enjoy.

BASIC
French Pie Crust

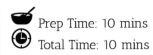

Prep Time: 10 mins
Total Time: 10 mins

Servings per Recipe: 8
Calories	155 kcal
Fat	8.8 g
Carbohydrates	17.5g
Protein	1.2 g
Cholesterol	0 mg
Sodium	161 mg

Ingredients

1 C. rice flour
1 tbsp white sugar
1/2 tsp salt
1/4 tsp baking powder

1/3 C. vegetable shortening
3 tbsp cold water
1/2 tsp vanilla extract

Directions

1. Set your oven to 375 degrees F before doing anything else.
2. In a bowl, mix together the rice flour, sugar, salt and baking powder.
3. Add the shortening and mix till the mixture resembles sand.
4. Stir in the water and vanilla extract.
5. Cook in the oven for about 5 minutes.

Waffles 101

 Prep Time: 10 mins

Total Time: 20 mins

Servings per Recipe: 5

Calories	278 kcal
Fat	18.5 g
Carbohydrates	22.6g
Protein	7.7 g
Cholesterol	80 mg
Sodium	815 mg

Ingredients

1 1/3 C. milk
1 C. buckwheat flour
1 C. almond flour
1/3 C. vegetable oil
2 eggs

1 tbsp baking powder
2 tsp white sugar
1 tsp salt

Directions

1. Set your waffle iron according to manufacturer's directions.
2. In a bowl, add the milk, buckwheat, almond flour, vegetable oil, eggs, baking powder, sugar and salt and mix till smooth.
3. Add the mixture into preheated waffle iron in batches and cook for about 3-5 minutes.

NEW AGE
Zucchini

Prep Time: 10 mins
Total Time: 15 mins

Servings per Recipe: 1
Calories	157 kcal
Fat	13.9 g
Carbohydrates	7.9 g
Protein	2.9 g
Cholesterol	0 mg
Sodium	181 mg

Ingredients

2 zucchinis, peeled
1 tbsp olive oil
1/4 C. water

salt and ground black pepper to taste

Directions

1. With a vegetable peeler, cut the zucchini in lengthwise slices, stopping when the seeds are reached.
2. Turn the zucchini over and peel till all the zucchini is in long strips.
3. Discard the seeds.
4. Now, slice the zucchini into thinner strips just like spaghetti.
5. In a skillet, heat the olive oil on medium heat and cook the zucchini for about 1 minute.
6. Add the water and cook for about 5-7 minutes.
7. Season with the salt and pepper and serve.

Creamy Mushroom 20 Minute Penne Dinner

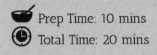 Prep Time: 10 mins

Total Time: 20 mins

Servings per Recipe: 6

Calories	482 kcal
Fat	26.8 g
Carbohydrates	51.9g
Protein	10 g
Cholesterol	60 mg
Sodium	217 mg

Ingredients

1 (12 oz.) box Barilla Gluten Free Penne
4 tbsp extra virgin olive oil
1/2 C. diced onion
1/2 lb. assorted mushrooms, sliced
1 C. heavy cream
1 C. peas

Salt and black pepper to taste
1/2 C. grated Parmigiano-Reggiano cheese

Directions

1. In large pan of the boiling water, prepare the pasta according to the package's directions.
2. Meanwhile in a large skillet, heat the olive oil and sauté the onion for about 5 minutes.
3. Add the heavy cream, peas, salt and pepper and bring to a simmer.
4. Drain the pasta well.
5. Immediately, add the hot pasta into the skillet with the sauce and stir to combine.
6. Remove from the heat and stir in the Parmigiano-Reggiano cheese.

BREAKFAST
Turkey Sandwich

Prep Time: 10 mins
Total Time: 15 mins

Servings per Recipe: 4

Calories	326.6
Fat	16.1g
Cholesterol	211.2mg
Sodium	675.2mg
Carbohydrates	29.2g
Protein	16.5g

Ingredients

8 slices turkey bacon, cut crosswise into strips
2 C. potatoes, shredded
2 large tomatoes, seeded and diced
1/4 C. dill pickle, diced
4 slices whole wheat bread, toasted

2 tbsp Smart Balance butter spread, melted
4 eggs
salt and pepper
salad greens

Directions

1. Place a pan over medium heat. Fry in it the bacon until it becomes crisp. Drain it and place it aside.
2. Stir the potato into the same pan with the bacon fat. Cook them until they become golden brown for about 4 min.
3. Stir in the tomatoes, dill pickle, and cooked bacon. Cook them for 2 min.
4. Place the toasted bread slices on a serving plate.
5. Spoon over them the potato and bacon mixture. Place it them aside.
6. Place a pan over medium heat. Heat in it the butter.
7. Crack in it eggs keeping each egg separate from the other. Season them with a pinch of salt and pepper.
8. Let them cook until they are done to your liking.
9. Place each fried egg on a sandwich. Serve them right away.
10. Enjoy.

Delaware
Inspires Chopped Salmon Sandwiches

Prep Time: 12 mins
Total Time: 20 mins

Servings per Recipe: 4
Calories   368.4
Fat   14.7g
Cholesterol   157.6mg
Sodium   1073.0mg
Carbohydrates   37.3g
Protein   21.1g

Ingredients

3 large eggs
1/3 C. mayonnaise
2 tsp horseradish, drained
8 slices rye bread
1/4 C. small mixed sprouts, such as radish
2 scallions, white and tender green parts only, sliced

4 large radishes, sliced
1/2 lb. sliced smoked salmon
salt & ground black pepper

Directions

1. Place a heavy saucepan over medium heat. Place in it the eggs and cover them with water.
2. Let them cook until they start boiling. put on the lid and turn off the heat.
3. Let them sit for 9 min. Drain and peel them. Roughly chop them.
4. Get a mixing bowl: Whisk in it the mayonnaise with horseradish.
5. Coat one side of the bread slices with it.
6. Place 4 slices of bread with the mayo side facing up on a serving plate.
7. Layover it the radish slices followed by sprouts, scallions, salmon, chopped eggs, a pinch of salt and pepper.*
8. Cover them with the remaining slices of bread. Slice your sandwiches in half then serve them.
9. Enjoy.

ATLANTA
Deli Sandwiches

Prep Time: 10 mins
Total Time: 20 mins

Servings per Recipe: 4
Calories	517.0
Fat	28.7g
Cholesterol	56.3mg
Sodium	1203.5mg
Carbohydrates	42.6g
Protein	22.9g

Ingredients

2 boneless chicken breasts
2 tbsp lemon pepper seasoning
1 tbsp olive oil
8 slices tomatoes
4 lettuce leaves
4 deli rolls

mayonnaise
1/2 C. ketchup
1/2 C. ranch dressing
1/4 C. prepared mustard

Directions

1. Get a mixing bowl: Whisk in it the ketchup, ranch dressing, and prepared mustard.
2. Place a large skillet over medium heat. Heat in it the oil.
3. Slice the chicken breasts in half lengthwise. Sprinkle on both sides lemon pepper seasonings.
4. Place them in the hot pan and cook them for 5 to 7 min on each side.
5. Coat the inside of the deli rolls with butter. Place them in a hot pan and toast them until they become golden.
6. Transfer them to a serving plate. Arrange over them the chicken breasts, lettuce, tomato, and ranch sauce.
7. Serve your sandwiches immediately.
8. Enjoy.

Venice Beach
Rolls

Prep Time: 15 mins
Total Time: 18 mins

Servings per Recipe: 4
Calories	438.3
Fat	21.7g
Cholesterol	66.1mg
Sodium	1166.2mg
Carbohydrates	36.6g
Protein	23.5g

Ingredients

8 oz. crabmeat, chopped
1/3 C. mayonnaise
1/4 C. celery, chopped
1/4 C. onion, chopped
1 tbsp prepared mustard
1/4 tsp seasoning salt

1/4 tsp curry powder
1/8 tsp pepper
4 rolls, split
1 C. cheddar cheese, shredded
1 tbsp butter, softened

Directions

1. Before you do anything, preheat the oven broiler.
2. Get a mixing bowl: Mix in it the crabmeat, mayonnaise, celery, onion, mustard, and seasonings.
3. Spoon 1/2 C. of the creamy mixture into each bread roll. Top it with cheese.
4. Coat the sandwiches with butter. Place them in the oven and toast them for 4 min.
5. Serve your sandwiches warm.
6. Enjoy.

RED PEPPER
Turkey Press

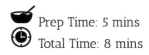

Prep Time: 5 mins
Total Time: 8 mins

Servings per Recipe: 1
Calories	794.5
Fat	27.4g
Cholesterol	125.2mg
Sodium	1020.9mg
Carbohydrates	83.4g
Protein	51.4g

Ingredients

2 slices sourdough bread
1 - 2 tbsp apricot jam
4 oz. sliced turkey breast
1 slice sweet onion
1/2 tbsp chopped roasted red pepper
2 slices swiss cheese

nonstick cooking spray

Directions

1. Place a pan over high heat. Grease it with a cooking spray.
2. Coat one side of a slice of bread. Place it aside.
3. Place the other slice of bread on a serving plate.
4. Top it with turkey, onion slice, roasted red peppers and swiss cheese.
5. Cover them with the second slice of the bread with the jam side facing down.
6. Place the sandwich in the hot pan. Put on the lid and cook them for 1 to 2 min on each side.
7. Serve your sandwiches warm.
8. Enjoy.

American Breakfast Sandwich

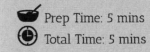

Prep Time: 5 mins
Total Time: 5 mins

Servings per Recipe: 1
Calories   513.6
Fat   28.9 g
Cholesterol   238.0mg
Sodium   1232.1mg
Carbohydrates   36.2 g
Protein   25.9 g

Ingredients

1 egg
1 slice bologna
1 slice cheese

1 kaiser roll

Directions

1. Place a skillet over medium heat. Heat in it a knob of butter.
2. Cook in it the bologna until it becomes golden brown. Drain it and place it aside.
3. Crack the egg in the same pan. Season it with a pinch of salt and pepper. Cook it until it is done.
4. Place the bologna slices in the bread rolls followed by the fried egg, and cheese.
5. Serve your sandwich right away.
6. Enjoy.

TOPPED
Turkey
Sandwiches

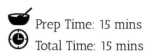

Prep Time: 15 mins

Total Time: 15 mins

Servings per Recipe: 4	
Calories	329.0
Fat	5.6g
Cholesterol	47.3mg
Sodium	398.4mg
Carbohydrates	46.5g
Protein	26.1g

Ingredients

1/4 C. slivered almonds
1/4 C. plain fat-free yogurt
3 tbsp low-fat mayonnaise
1 tsp bottled ground ginger
1/8 tsp crushed red pepper flakes
3/4 C. sliced celery
1/4 C. chopped red onion
1/4 C. dried cherries

1/4 C. golden raisin
8 oz. roast cooked turkey breast, chopped
4 whole wheat pita bread, halved

Directions

1. Place a pan over medium heat. Toast in it the almonds for 2 to 3 min. Place them aside to cool down.

2. Get a mixing bowl: Mix in it the rest of the ingredients with almonds.

3. Divide the mixture between the pita halves. Serve them.

4. Enjoy.

Tahini
Sandwich

Prep Time: 5 mins
Total Time: 7 mins

Servings per Recipe: 1
Calories	375.6
Fat	12.4g
Cholesterol	0.0mg
Sodium	333.2mg
Carbohydrates	63.2g
Protein	9.8g

Ingredients

1 small apple, cored and sliced
1 tsp peanut butter
2 slices whole wheat bread
1 tbsp tahini
1 tbsp honey

1/4 tsp cinnamon

Directions

1. Coat one side of a slice of bread with peanut butter.
2. Arrange over it the apple slices followed by tahini, honey, and cinnamon.
3. Cover them with the second slice of bread. Place the sandwich in a hot pan and toast it for 1 min on each side.
4. Serve your sandwich with some tea.
5. Enjoy.

6-MINUTE
Windy City Sandwich (Italian Beef)

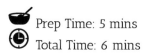

Prep Time: 5 mins
Total Time: 6 mins

Servings per Recipe: 1
Calories	304.5
Fat	16.9g
Cholesterol	107.7mg
Sodium	307.6mg
Carbohydrates	0.6g
Protein	37.4g

Ingredients

1 (10 1/2 oz.) cans au jus sauce
1 sourdough roll
4 oz. thin-sliced roast beef
1/4 C. giardiniera, drained and chopped

1 slice provolone cheese
butter

Directions

1. Place a small saucepan over medium heat. Stir in it the beef au jjus sauce for 4 min.
2. Coat the inside of the bread roll with butter.
3. Place a pan over medium heat. Place in it the roll with the open facing down.
4. Toast it for 1 to 2 min until it becomes golden.
5. Place the bread roll on a serving plate. Spoon into it the hot beef mixture followed by giardiniera and cheese.
6. Place the roll back in the pan and cover it. Let it cook over low heat until the cheese melts.
7. Serve your sandwiches warm.
8. Enjoy.

Weeknight Ground Beef Sandwiches

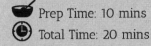 Prep Time: 10 mins

Total Time: 20 mins

Servings per Recipe: 1
Calories	176.7
Fat	8.1g
Cholesterol	49.4mg
Sodium	165.4mg
Carbohydrates	13.9g
Protein	11.1g

Ingredients

1 lb. ground beef
1 large egg
1 onion, chopped
1 tbsp dried thyme
salt
ground black pepper

ground cumin
ground coriander
ground ginger
10 slices bread

Directions

1. Before you do anything, preheat the oven to 350 F.
2. Get a large mixing bowl: Mix in it the beef, egg, onion, thyme, black pepper, cumin, coriander, and ginger.
3. Place the bread slices on a baking tray. Spoon into them the beef mixture and spread it.
4. Cook the sandwiches in the oven for 6 to 11 min. Serve them warm.
5. Enjoy.

CHEESY
French Toast Sandwiches

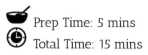 Prep Time: 5 mins

Total Time: 15 mins

Servings per Recipe: 4
Calories
Fat   371.9
Cholesterol   22.7g
Sodium   160.8mg
Carbohydrates   911.3mg
Protein   26.8g

Ingredients

2 eggs
1/3 C. milk
1/2 tsp salt
8 slices white bread

mustard, prepared
4 slices cheddar cheese, sliced
3 tbsp butter

Directions

1. Get a shallow bowl: Whisk in it the eggs with milk and a pinch of salt.
2. Coat the side facing up of 4 bread slices with mustard. Top them with cheddar cheese.
3. Coat one side of the remaining slices with mayo and place it on top with the mayo side facing down.
4. Place a large pan over medium heat. Heat in it the butter.
5. Dip the sandwiches in the egg mixture. Cook them in the hot pan for 3 to 4 min on each side.
6. Serve your sandwiches warm with extra toppings if you desire.
7. Enjoy.

Pepperjack
Sourdoughs

Prep Time: 10 mins
Total Time: 20 mins

Servings per Recipe: 2
Calories   488.3
Fat   10.1g
Cholesterol   53.5mg
Sodium   837.4mg
Carbohydrates   66.5g
Protein   31.4g

Ingredients

4 slices thick sourdough bread
1/3 lb. sliced roast beef
4 slices monterey jack with jalapeno
pepper cheese, sliced
1 tsp canned diced green chilies
mayonnaise

melted butter
salt

Directions

1. Brush one side of the bread slices with butter.

2. Place 2 of them on a cutting board. Top them with mayo, beef slices, and 1/2 tsp of green chilies.

3. Coat the other side of the remaining bread slices with mayo.

4. Place them over the sandwiches with the mayo side facing down.

5. Place a large pan over medium heat. Toast in it the sandwiches for 2 to 3 min on each side.

6. Serve them warm.

7. Enjoy.

HONEY
Peanut Butter Sandwich

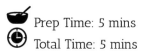

Prep Time: 5 mins
Total Time: 5 mins

Servings per Recipe: 1
Calories	257.7
Fat	10.2g
Cholesterol	0.0mg
Sodium	280.8mg
Carbohydrates	36.3g
Protein	7.9g

Ingredients

2 slices cinnamon raisin bread
1 -2 tbsp chunky peanut butter
1 tsp honey

Directions

1. Place a slice of bread on a serving plate.
2. Top it with peanut butter and honey. Cover it with the second slice of bread
3. Serve your classic sandwich right away.
4. Enjoy.

Portuguese Inspired Pimento Sandwiches

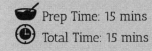 Prep Time: 15 mins

Total Time: 15 mins

Servings per Recipe: 4
Calories   355.1
Fat   20.4g
Cholesterol   3.8mg
Sodium   491.0mg
Carbohydrates   35.1g
Protein   11.0g

Ingredients

3 large carrots, peeled, shredded
2/3 C. walnuts, ground
8 green olives, minced
1 tbsp pimiento, chopped
1 garlic clove, minced
1/4-1/2 C. mayonnaise

1 tbsp basil, chopped, dried
8 slices whole grain bread

Directions

1. Get a mixing bowl: Stir in it the walnuts with garlic, carrots, mayo, a pinch of salt and pepper.
2. Stir in the basil.
3. Coat one side of each bread slice with some mayo.
4. Top 4 of them with the carrot mixture. Cover them with the remaining bread slices.
5. Slice the sandwiches in half the serve them.
6. Enjoy.

LATE
October
Sandwiches

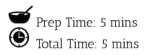
Prep Time: 5 mins

Total Time: 5 mins

Servings per Recipe: 2
Calories	577.6
Fat	34.6g
Cholesterol	0.0mg
Sodium	561.2mg
Carbohydrates	51.1g
Protein	24.3g

Ingredients

1/2 C. pumpkin
1/2 C. peanut butter
4 slices whole wheat bread

1 medium banana, sliced

Directions

1. Get a mixing bowl: Beat in it the pumpkin with peanut butter until they become creamy.
2. Lay 2 slices of bread on a serving plate. Top them with some of the pumpkin butter and banana slices.
3. Cover them with the rest of the bread slices. Serve them.
4. Enjoy.

Fruity Tuna Sandwiches

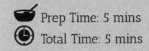 Prep Time: 5 mins

Total Time: 5 mins

Servings per Recipe: 6
Calories	271.5
Fat	4.5g
Cholesterol	35.7mg
Sodium	599.4mg
Carbohydrates	28.8g
Protein	27.9g

Ingredients

18 oz. solid white tuna packed in water, drained
1/3 C. dried sweetened cranberries
1 celery rib, chopped
1/2 C. mayonnaise

1 hard-cooked egg white, chopped
12 slices whole wheat bread

Directions

1. Get a mixing bowl: Combine in it the tuna with cranberries, celery, mayo, and chopped egg.
2. Season them with a pinch of salt and pepper.
3. Place 6 slices of bread on a serving plate. Spoon into them the tuna mixture.
4. Cover them with the rest of the bread slices. Serve your sandwiches immediately.
5. Enjoy.

HOW TO MAKE
a Quiche Crust

Prep Time: 10 mins
Total Time: 20 mins

Servings per Recipe: 6

Calories	178 kcal
Carbohydrates	12 g
Cholesterol	35 mg
Fat	13.2 g
Protein	2.9 g
Sodium	111 mg

Ingredients

3/4 cup all-purpose flour
6 tbsps cold butter, cut into small pieces
1/4 cup shredded Cheddar cheese

5 tsps cold water

Directions

1. Preheat your oven at 350 degrees F and put some oil over the quiche dish.
2. Combine flour and butter in a bowl very thoroughly before adding grated cheese.
3. Add water spoon after spoon until you can form a ball out of it.
4. Wrap this dough with plastic wrap before refrigerating it for at least thirty minutes.
5. Roll this dough and put this in the quiche dish.
6. Bake in the preheated oven for about 10 minutes before filling it with quiche custard of your choice.

Creamy
Olive Omelet

Prep Time: 10 mins
Total Time: 20 mins

Servings per Recipe: 2
Calories	627 kcal
Fat	46.6 g
Carbohydrates	10.8g
Protein	40.6 g
Cholesterol	419 mg
Sodium	740 mg

Ingredients

2 tsp vegetable oil
1/2 small onion, chopped
1 (5 oz.) can tuna, drained
1/3 C. sour cream
3 tbsp cream cheese
1/2 C. shredded mozzarella cheese
1 (2.25 oz.) can sliced black olives

1/8 tsp dried dill weed
1/8 tsp garlic powder
5 eggs
1/4 C. milk
2 tsp vegetable oil

Directions

1. In a large skillet, heat 2 tsp of the vegetable oil on medium heat and cook the onion till it begins to brown.
2. In a large bowl, mix together the tuna, cream cheese, sour cream, mozzarella cheese, olives, dill, garlic powder and cooked onion
3. In a large bowl, add the eggs and milk and beat well.
4. In the same skillet, heat 2 tsp of the oil and cook the egg mixture till set, lifting the edges occasionally.
5. Place the tuna mixture over one half of the omelet and fold the over the filling.
6. Cover the pan and remove from the heat.
7. Keep aside, covered pan till cheese is melted.

THURSDAY'S
Lunch Box (Pasta with Capers)

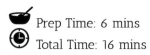 Prep Time: 6 mins

Total Time: 16 mins

Servings per Recipe: 4

Calories	641.8
Fat	6.1g
Cholesterol	14.3mg
Sodium	196.3mg
Carbohydrates	112.4g
Protein	31.9g

Ingredients

17.5 oz. spaghetti
6.5 cans tuna in olive oil, drained
15.5 oz. cans of peeled roma tomatoes, diced
1 small white onion, diced
sea salt

crushed black peppercorns
capers
grated parmesan cheese

Directions

1. Prepare the pasta by following the instructions on the package.
2. Place a pan over medium heat. Heat in it a splash of oil. Cook in it the onion with tuna for 3 min.
3. Add the tomato and cook them for 3 min. Stir in the tuna with capers.
4. Divide the spaghetti between serving plates. Spoon over it the tuna mixture.
5. Sprinkle the cheese on top then serve them.
6. Enjoy.

Spaghetti Kalamata

Prep Time: 20 mins
Total Time: 20 mins

Servings per Recipe: 4
Calories   627.5
Fat   29.8g
Cholesterol   25.3mg
Sodium   793.9mg
Carbohydrates   74.0g
Protein   17.2g

Ingredients

1 1/2 lbs. tomatoes, seeded and chopped
1/2 C. kalamata olives, pitted
1/4 lb. feta cheese, crumbled
3 tbsp capers, drained
3 tbsp flat leaf parsley, chopped
1/4 tsp salt

1/4 tsp fresh ground black pepper
3/4 lb. spaghetti
6 tbsp olive oil
3 garlic cloves, minced

Directions

1. Prepare the spaghetti by following the instructions on the package.
2. Get a mixing bowl: Combine in it the tomatoes, olives, feta, capers, parsley, salt, and pepper.
3. Place a pan over medium heat. Heat in it the oil. Cook in it the garlic for 60 seconds.
4. Stir in the spaghetti and toss them to coat. Add the tomato mixture and toss to coat.
5. Adjust the seasoning of the salad then let it chill in the fridge for at least 1 h.
6. Serve your salad with some garlic bread.
7. Enjoy.

WEST VIRGINIA
French Toast Waffles

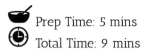

Prep Time: 5 mins
Total Time: 9 mins

Servings per Recipe: 2
Calories	329.3
Fat	19.2g
Cholesterol	246.3mg
Sodium	507.2mg
Carbohydrates	27.1g
Protein	11.2g

Ingredients

4 -6 slices thick-sliced bread, trimmed
2 eggs, beaten
1/4 C. milk
2 tbsp butter, melted

1/4 tsp vanilla
1/4 tsp cinnamon

Directions

1. Set your waffle iron and lightly, grease it.
2. In a shallow dish, add the butter, milk, eggs, vanilla and cinnamon and beat until well combined.
3. Coat each bread slices with egg mixture evenly.
4. Arrange the bread slices in waffle iron and cook until golden brown.
5. Enjoy warm with a topping of your favorite condiments.

Kentucky
Blueberry Waffles

Prep Time: 10 mins
Total Time: 20 mins

Servings per Recipe: 1

Calories	305.7
Fat	11.9g
Cholesterol	90.8mg
Sodium	497.5mg
Carbohydrates	40.9g
Protein	8.6g

Ingredients

1 C. blueberries
3 tsp baking powder
2 eggs, separated
1 tbsp sugar
2 C. sifted flour

1 1/2 C. milk
1/2 tsp salt
1/4 C. melted butter

Directions

1. Set your waffle iron and lightly, grease it.
2. In a glass bowl, add the egg whites and beat until stiff peak form.
3. In a bowl, add the flour, baking powder and salt and mix well.
4. Now, sift the flour mixture in a second bowl.
5. In a third bowl, add the butter, egg yolks and milk and beat until well combined.
6. Slowly, add the butter mixture into the flour mixture, beating continuously until well combined.
7. Add the blueberries and gently, stir to combine.
8. Gently, fold the whipped egg whites into the flour mixture.
9. Add desired amount of the mixture in waffle iron and cook as suggested by the manufacturer.
10. Repeat with the remaining mixture.
11. Enjoy warm.

ENHANCED
Toasted Waffles

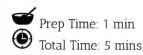 Prep Time: 1 min
Total Time: 5 mins

Servings per Recipe: 4
Calories   576.0
Fat   28.4g
Cholesterol   126.9mg
Sodium   840.8mg
Carbohydrates   68.0g
Protein   13.5g

Ingredients

8 frozen waffles, toasted
3 oz. cream cheese
14 oz. canned peaches
1 tbsp brown sugar

whipped cream

Directions

1. Spread cream cheese over each toasted waffle, followed by the fruit, brown sugar and whipped cream.
2. Enjoy.

Ice Cream
Waffle Sandwiches

Prep Time: 5 mins
Total Time: 7 mins

Servings per Recipe: 1
Calories	709.7
Fat	35.6g
Cholesterol	161.5mg
Sodium	872.1mg
Carbohydrates	80.5g
Protein	16.4g

Ingredients

2 toasted hot waffles
1 C. ice cream
Toppings
1 - 2 tbsp decorative candies
1 - 2 tbsp crushed nuts
1 - 2 tbsp toasted coconut
1 - 2 tbsp granola cereal

1 - 2 tbsp praline
peanut butter spread on before ice cream

Directions

1. Place a thin layer of the peanut butter over each waffle evenly.
2. Put the ice cream onto inner part of each waffle.
3. Place your favorite topping beside the ice cream.
4. Enjoy.

COUNTRY
Cottage Waffles

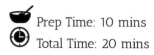

Prep Time: 10 mins
Total Time: 20 mins

Servings per Recipe: 1
Calories	312.1
Fat	12.6g
Cholesterol	94.0mg
Sodium	540.3mg
Carbohydrates	38.6g
Protein	11.1g

Ingredients

4 tbsp unsalted butter, melted
1 3/4 C. all-purpose flour
2 tsp baking powder
1/4 tsp baking soda
1/2 tsp salt
1 C. cottage cheese

1 C. milk
2 large eggs
2 1/2 tbsp honey

Directions

1. Set your waffle iron and lightly, grease it.
2. In a bowl, add the flour, baking powder, baking soda and salt and mix well.
3. In another bowl, add the honey, eggs, milk and cottage cheese and beat until just combined.
4. Slowly, add the flour mixture and mix until just combined.
5. Add the butter and stir to combine.
6. Add desired amount of the mixture in waffle iron and cook as suggested by the manufacturer.
7. Repeat with the remaining mixture.
8. Enjoy warm.

ENJOY THE RECIPES?

KEEP ON COOKING
WITH 6 MORE FREE COOKBOOKS!

Visit our website and simply enter your email address to join the club and receive your 6 cookbooks.

http://booksumo.com/magnet

https://www.instagram.com/booksumopress/

https://www.facebook.com/booksumo/

Printed in Great Britain
by Amazon